What if I'm Wrong?

Previous Books:

Exposed to Winds
[Selected poems]

Construction Delay Claims

Anecdotes of Would-be Experts

Thoughts in a Maze

Trials and Errors, Laughs & Terrors

Characters

Oddities

Connections

Conclusions Volumes I & II

My Best Dog Days

Investment Fundamentals

Our Support Systems

About My Books

Human Traits & Follies

Honesty's Travesty

Critical Reflections

Us Ordinary Folk

Short Short Stories

Imagined Realities

What if I'm Wrong?

by

Arthur O.R. Thormann

Specfab Industries Ltd.

Edmonton, Alberta

2020

Thormann, Arthur O. R. (Arthur Otto Rudolf), 1934-, author
    What if I'm Wrong?

ISBN 978-1-7770735-0-3

Copyright © Arthur O.R. Thormann, 2020

Publisher: Specfab Industries Ltd.
                     13559 - 123A Avenue
                     Edmonton, Alberta, Canada
                     T5L 2Z1
                     Telephone: 780-454-6396

Publication assistance by

PAGEMASTER
PUBLISHING
PageMaster.ca

Cover Designs: Front: Image: a thinking emoji
                    Back: Text by author; image: a shocked emoji

Questionable Belief:
Why do you believe
That all of our grief
Will soon be over
And we'll be in clover?
What if you're wrong?

I dedicate this book to those who want
to shed their prejudices!

My gratitude also goes to my daughters
Nancy & Diana for their valued edits.
All mistakes remaining are mine.

Author's Note

Our world is filled with questionable beliefs and prejudices. To rid ourselves of prejudices, it is wise to seriously ask the question, "What if I'm wrong?"

This book is about our current affairs that require such a question. I'll leave the answers up to you.

Arthur O.R. Thormann
January 2020

Contents

Introduction

All my life I was, still am, a firm proponent of eliminating prejudice and bias in the world. Many years ago, I accidentally stumbled onto the question "What if I'm wrong?" and I realized immediately that this question could accomplish the difficult task – not just by saying the words, but by sincerely questioning one's belief even in the face of overwhelming evidence to support it. The same question applies on a wider scale: "What if he/she, we/they are wrong?" Question everything and everybody.

Here is an example of the wider-scale question from a novel by Lawrence Sanders called *McNally's Secret*, where his protagonist Archibald McNally contemplates:

> "...In my going-on thirty-seven years I have lived through dire warnings of nuclear catastrophe, global warming, ozone depletion, universal extinction via cholesterol, and the invasion of killer bees.
>
> After a while my juices stopped their panicky surge and I realized I was bored with all

these screeched predictions of Armageddon due next Tuesday. It hadn't happened yet, had it? The old world tottered along, and I was content to totter along with it. I am an amiable, sunnily tempered chap (and something of an ass, my father would undoubtedly add), and I see no need to concern myself with disasters that may never happen. The world is filled with kvetchers, and I have no desire to join the club."

Evidently, what is going through Archibald McNally's (Lawrence Sanders's) mind is the question "What if they are wrong?"

Beliefs should be backed up by facts! Otherwise, one could definitely be wrong!

Now take one or more of your beliefs – I'll give you some examples that may or may not apply to you: whites are better than blacks; blacks are better than whites; women are better than men; men are better than women; juniors are smarter than seniors; people attain wisdom only at old age; I can sin because Jesus died for my sins; God is a gentle, loving old man. who will look after me if I pray hard enough; my body will perish, but my soul will live on; I may leave this planet, but I will return to live another life; if I sin, Satan will inherit my soul; I can walk across the street without watching the traffic, because my guardian angel will protect me – and ask yourself "What if I'm wrong?" Don't just say the words, but engage in some serious examinations.

Scientists' beliefs can also come in question. Albert Einstein believed that nothing is faster than light. I'm not a scientist, so I'm not going to trouble you with the theory of tachyons, but let's take a look at the light that comes from our sun. Earth's average distance from the sun is 92,960,000 miles, and light travels at 186,282 miles per second; therefore, it takes light 499 seconds to reach Earth from the sun, or almost eight and a third minutes. Can anything travel faster than that? Yes. Take our thoughts: our thoughts can reach the sun in a split-second, and that is much faster than light. Could I be wrong? Well, someone could say that all I see when I look at the sun is the light emitted from it, which took eight and one-third minutes to reach us, and eight and one-third minutes earlier the sun could have looked different (sun spots that might have disappeared in eight and one-third minutes, etc.) which I didn't see, and, therefore, my thoughts could not travel faster than light. Does that make sense to you? No? Well, it all comes down to the question "Could he be wrong?" does it not?

When our leaders go wrong, we're in serious trouble.

Adolf Hitler was one of many twentieth century

leaders who should have asked himself the question "What if I'm wrong?" He was a mere corporal in the German Army at the end of the First World War, but he considered Germany's surrender a political rather than a military defeat. Also, he considered the Treaty of Versailles nothing short of treason against the German people, both by the Allies as well as the German officials who signed it. He promised himself that if he was ever given the opportunity he would reverse the severe conditions of this Treaty! What followed was one of the biggest blood baths in human history!

Twenty-first century leaders must ask themselves the question, too. Take David Cameron. When his Conservatives secured an unexpected majority in the 2015 general election, he remained as Prime Minister. To fulfil a manifesto pledge, he introduced a referendum on the UK's continuing membership of the EU. Cameron supported continued membership, but following the success of the Leave vote, he resigned and was succeeded by Theresa May. Had Cameron asked himself the question he may not have introduced the referendum.

In the following chapters, I intend to explore some of the mistakes our leaders can and do make when they fail to ask themselves "What if I'm wrong?"

Impeachment

In the context of this chapter, I shall use Merriam-Webster's dictionary definition for impeachment: to charge (a public official) before a competent tribunal with misconduct in office, and the Wikipedia: Impeachment is the process by which a legislative body levels charges against a government official. Impeachment does not in itself remove the official definitively from office; it is similar to an indictment in criminal law, and thus it is essentially the statement of charges against the official.

In US President Donald Trump's case, according to the Wikipedia, a formal impeachment inquiry was launched on September 24, 2019, as a response to the Trump–Ukraine scandal, in which Trump and his personal attorney Rudy Giuliani pressed the Ukrainian government repeatedly since at least May, 2019, to investigate Hunter Biden, the son of 2020 presidential candidate Joe Biden. The purpose of the requested investigation was alleged to be to hurt Biden's campaign for President. In July Trump issued a hold on military aid scheduled to send to Ukraine, releasing it in September after controversy arose. There was widespread speculation that the withholding of the aid was intended to force Ukraine to investigate Biden; both Trump and Giuliani seemed to confirm that there was such a connection. As of October 19, 2019, out of a total of 432 incumbent members of the House of Representatives, 228 Democrats and one independent are on the record as supporting the launch of an impeachment inquiry.

How difficult is it to be a US president and keep your nose clean? A vast extent of backup is available to the president, so, I think any normally intelligent person could do the job; it's not that difficult. Meals are looked after; all personal needs are looked after; all requests are immediately satisfied; the body is protected at all times; at the daily briefing, important new developments are discussed, and necessary actions are being sanctioned; all critical decisions are aided by competent advisors; unknown territories are cleared up by enlightened experts; all the president has to do is use his sound judgement to agree with his educated advisors; foreign policy is governed by historic precedence, and seldom presents any problems for the president; for unpopular issues, like abortion and assisted suicides, the president can hide behind established laws rather than voice his own religious beliefs; much of what the president can opine in this regard is guided by his party's campaign platform; if the president goes along with his expert advisors, he will seldom go wrong, and if he is in doubt, just ask the question: "What if I'm wrong?"

But Donald Trump, the 45th president of the USA, has difficulties doing that, and that is what got him into impeachment procedures against him. Donald Trump's forthright assertions, even some lies, have made him a few enemies, but many of the people love him, because they feel he is one of them.

Here is what CNN reports: Nancy Pelosi, Speaker of the United States House of Representatives, was against Trump's impeachment for the longest time; Pelosi was concerned about voters' appetite for a lengthy process: "How much drama can the American people handle?" but Trump's Ukrainian escapade changed her mind. Nancy Pelosi wants people to know that the House Democratic leadership has not committed to impeaching President Donald Trump — notwithstanding the muscle she's thrown behind the inquiry, but she believes the House Intelligence Committee's investigation has already accumulated enough evidence about Trump's pressure campaign on Ukraine to justify such a decision. She was equally unequivocal that the core charges against Trump — that he withheld congressionally appropriated military aid to try to force Ukraine to investigate a political opponent — reach the standard of "high crimes and misdemeanors" required for impeachment. She said, "We might as well not even run for office. You don't need this branch of government if he's going to overturn the power of the purse, if he is going to overturn all of the other checks and balances, the power of inquiry. When we decide if we are going to go forward, we will be ready, and we will be ironclad," referring to potential votes on articles of impeachment. "In saying that he wasn't going to send the military assistance to Ukraine, who benefits from that? The Russians. Then … he did what he did in Syria — who benefits from that? Putin. What he said earlier about NATO — who benefits from that? Putin," she said. "That's what I was saying the other day: 'All roads lead to Putin.'"

"The times have found us," Nancy Pelosi said, "to protect this Constitution of the United States with three co-equal branches of government as a check and balance on each other."

Pelosi is a wise lady; if I were the president, I would want her on my side and seek her advice.

However, it appears that Trump's impeachment is more of a partisan issue than a wrong versus right issue. Half the American people think Trump acted properly, the other half think he acted wrongly. How can such a division be adequately adjudicated? What if half the American people are wrong?

Referendums

I have already mentioned in my previous books that referendums are prone to failure, that is, failure as far as a true opinion is concerned. People who vote on referendums seldom know the implications, and why should they? They have elected representatives who should know what these implications are. But their representatives, out of cowardice, went back to the voters. If the voters are wrong, the representatives cannot be blamed, can they? And so, partially out of ignorance, voters will make decisions in referendums that often come back to haunt them! And that is what happened, for example, in the Brexit and other referendums!

At one time, I voted on a referendum that wanted to get rid of the municipal airport in the center of Edmonton, Alberta. Most people who voted never used this airport, and some people did not even know that there was such an airport. The mayor of Edmonton was in favor of getting rid of the airport, thus, the ignorant voters also voted in favor, believing that the mayor knows best, but it turned out that the mayor did not know best! A few months later, when other issues about getting rid of this airport became evident, the mayor sadly announced that the referendum vote had been a "mistake!" but the wrong decision had become irreversible!

Some of the following paragraphs are from the New York Times, under the heading: Why Referendums Aren't as Democratic as They Seem, by Amanda Taub and Max Fisher, October 4, 2016: The voters of the world have had quite a year: They rejected Colombia's peace deal; split Britain from the European Union; endorsed a Thai Constitution that curtails democracy; and, in Hungary, backed the government's plan to restrict refugees, but without the necessary turnout for a valid result. Each of these moves was determined by a national referendum. Though voters upended their governments' plans, eroded their own rights, and ignited political crises, they all accomplished one thing: They demonstrated why many political scientists consider referendums messy and dangerous.

When asked whether referendums were a good idea, Michael Marsh, a political scientist at Trinity College Dublin, said, "The simple answer is almost never." – "I've watched many of these in Ireland, and they really range from the pointless to the dangerous," he added.

Though such votes are portrayed as popular

governance in its purest form, studies have found that they often subvert democracy rather than serve it. They tend to be volatile, turning not just on the merits of the decision but also on unrelated political swings or even, as may have happened in Colombia, on the weather. Voters must make their decisions with relatively little information, forcing them to rely on political messaging — which puts power in the hands of political elites rather than those of voters.

Voters face a problem in any referendum: They need to distill difficult policy choices down to a simple yes or no, and predict the outcome of decisions so complex that even experts might spend years struggling to understand them. When a referendum is put forward by the government, people often vote in support if they like the leadership and vote in opposition if they dislike it, according to research by Lawrence LeDuc, a political scientist and professor emeritus at the University of Toronto.

In Britain's debate over whether to leave the European Union, or "Brexit," neither side emphasized the specifics of membership in the bloc, instead framing the vote as a choice about which values to emphasize. The "Remain" campaign presented membership as a matter of economic stability. The "Leave" campaign emphasized immigration issues. It worked. People who voted to remain expressed great concern about the economy, but not much about immigrants. People who voted to leave said they were very concerned about immigration, and less so about the economy. The voters of neither side asked, "What if I'm wrong?"

And so, three-and-a-half years after the Brexit referendum, Brexit is not yet concluded, and the British populace is being asked to vote again, this time for a government that is able, hopefully, to negotiate the divorce from the EU to everyone's satisfaction.

An alternative to a referendum is for the government to appoint a nonpartisan commission of experts who are familiar with the pros and cons of the issue to be decided. These experts would discuss the issue and assign weight to each pro and con, and based on the outcome of these weights they would give their recommendation to the government. The government would then make its decision and inform the populace of the method it had used to reach the decision.

In the case of Brexit, the conclusion of such a commission is highly speculative at this point, but, at least, it would have been an informed conclusion, reached by nonpartisan experts; their conclusion may well have been equally divided between the weights of the pros and cons, in which case the government would have been forced to add its own weight, based on political considerations.

Trade Wars

Trade wars are standard between business competitors, and these business trade wars go back thousands of years, but trade wars between nations go back only hundreds of years, sometimes involving violence, and seldom benefitting the populations of these nations. Trade wars in business are important to progressive activities. Monopolies suppress progressive activities and should be discouraged. When the necessity to meet competition is removed, the necessity to become innovative is also removed.

Trade wars between nations are much more serious than trade wars between companies. Take the Anglo-Dutch trade wars. Three of these wars, mostly naval battles between England and the Dutch Republic, were fought during the second half of the seventeenth century over trade and overseas colonies. They were fought at sea, and both sides suffered heavy losses. Then, after England and the Dutch Republic were allied for a century, they went to war again in 1780–84, over secret Dutch trade and negotiations with the American colonies – the American colonies were revolting against England at the time. When the war finally ended in 1784, the Dutch were at the lowest point of their power and prestige.

The next trade war between nations took place in China, known as the Opium Wars. There were two wars, the first to decide the issue of China's attempt to suppress the opium trade. Primarily, British traders had been illegally exporting opium, mainly from India to China. The resulting widespread addiction in China was causing social and economic disruptions. In 1839, the Chinese government confiscated about 1,400 tons of opium that was warehoused by British merchants in Canton. Hostilities broke out that year when British warships destroyed a Chinese blockade at the Pearl River estuary of Hong Kong. Despite counterattacks by Chinese troops in 1842, the British held against the offense, and peace negotiations followed. The Chinese were then required to pay the British a large indemnity, cede the Hong Kong Island to the British, and increase the number of ports where the British could trade and reside. During the second war, fourteen years later, the British were aided by French forces. Both wars and subsequently imposed treaties substantially weakened the Qing dynasty and the Chinese governments.

At the end of the nineteenth century, the United States of America started the Banana Wars, which consisted of occupations, police actions, and interventions by the USA in Central America and the Caribbean, and ended in 1934 with the inception of the Good Neighbor Policy.

Then, in 1930, the USA passed the Smoot–Hawley Tariff Act, which added US tariffs on more than 20,000 imported goods.

From 1932-1938 the Anglo-Irish Trade War took place. The Irish Free State withheld land annuity payments to the United Kingdom for land purchases prior to independence, and the UK retaliated with duties on Irish food products to the UK. Then, the Irish retaliated with restrictions on coal, steel, cement, and other imports from Britain, and the tit-for-tat that followed led to a severe deterioration of Anglo-Irish relations. It ended with the signing of a trade agreement in 1938 that involved a sizeable generosity on part of the UK.

In the twenty-first century, during 2010-2011, an international trade war developed between food-exporting nations over genetically modified food. For example, in 2010, Canadian flax exports to Europe were rejected when traces of experimental, genetically modified flax were found in shipments. According to scientific consensus, food derived from genetically modified crops poses no greater risk to human health than conventional food, providing it is properly tested on a case-by-case basis before introduction.

Then, in 2018, the United States President Donald Trump imposed a number of tariffs on other countries' products as part of his "America First" economic policy to reduce the US trade deficit and shifted from multilateral free-trade agreements to bilateral deals. President Donald Trump also started the China-United States trade war by setting tariffs and other trade barriers on China with the goal of changing "unfair trade practices." China, of course, retaliated with its own tariffs on American goods.

When tariffs are involved in nations' trade war, Nation A will add a money amount to the products imported from Nation B, and this added money amount is called a tariff, which is like a government sales tax on foreign products; it is intended to bring the prices of the foreign products equal or higher than the prices of the domestic products. Then, to retaliate, Nation B will add a money amount to the products imported from Nation A. In the end, both of the populations of Nation A and Nation B lose because they must pay higher prices for these products. Does this kind of trade war make sense? I'm not well enough educated in economic theories to answer this question, but it seems to make sense to some politicians like Donald Trump. Still, I wonder if Donald Trump ever asks himself, "what if I'm wrong?"

Brexit

Regardless of economic respects, one must consider the pride of the British people to understand Brexit. A mere hundred years ago, Great Britain was still a world power, and with her membership in the European Union she must subject herself to the laws and rules of other nations – other nations whom she has conquered in the past. This does not sit well with her people, at least not with half her people. The other half of her people are more concerned with the benefits of being part of the European Union. So, one half supports the reasons to leave, and the other half supports the reasons to stay in the European Union, but the decision is slightly more in favor of leaving. However, leaving is not as simple as walking away. Economic as well as political issues must be resolved.

Britain was already aloof from Continental Europe's first effort towards integration after World War II, i.e., the European Coal and Steel Community (ECSC) and the European Economic Community (EEC) formed to avoid another devastating war. Eventually, Britain wanted to join the EEC, but French President Charles de Gaulle opposed Britain's application. In his address to an audience at the Élysée Palace in 1967, he said that the British view of European construction was characterized by a deep-seated hostility and that the UK would require a radical transformation if it were ever to be allowed to join the Common Market. The UK wrote an indignant reply to President de Gaulle, but it was to no avail. The UK's application for membership in the EEC was not approved until Charles de Gaulle fell from power, in fact not until de Gaulle died. The UK joined the EEC in 1973, and the British people approved the membership in a 1975 referendum, but their suspicion of a political union with the rest of Europe remained strong.

And as integration deepened during the 1980s and 1990s, the British leadership pushed more and more for opt outs. The UK didn't join the single currency, or the border-free Schengen Area (free movement in Europe). The UK also negotiated a reduced budget contribution. Nevertheless, many conservatives could not reconcile with membership in the European Union, and discontent rose especially over immigration. When economic migration from Eastern Europe spiked after the European Union's expansion and pushed it to more than 300,000 per year to the UK by 2015, the UK Prime Minister David Cameron called it unsustainable.

In a 2013 speech, David Cameron had attacked flaws in the Eurozone, and promised to hold a referendum on the UK's membership in the European Union if the Conservative Party won the 2015 election. Then, in November 2015, David Cameron announced that before holding a referendum he would seek European Union reform in four areas: national sovereignty, immigration policy, financial and economic regulation, and competitiveness. In February 2016, European Union leaders agreed to a number of changes, including official recognition that the push for "ever closer union" does not apply to the UK, but the unresolved migration issue gave the leave camp the ammunition it needed.

On 23 June 2016, the British people settled the question with a leave vote in their referendum. Given a free hand, David Cameron would not have wanted to hold a referendum, but having called the vote, he vowed to campaign with his "heart and soul" to keep Britain in the European Union. However, when the leave campaign won at 51.9%, David Cameron announced his resignation the following day, and former home secretary Theresa May took over one of the most tumultuous premiership in history, with Brexit overshadowing all other issues for the next three years.

Theresa May is a serious British woman who was

seriously intent to accomplish Brexit for the British people who voted leave in the referendum. When she ran into difficulties, she could have held another referendum, but she refused to do so out of respect for the people who voted for leave. After invoking the EU's Article 50 in March 2017, she spent more than a year negotiating a withdrawal agreement with EU leaders. She finally reached a deal late in 2018, and on 15 January 2019 the British Parliament overwhelmingly rejected the 585-page treaty she had proposed. Two further votes on it also saw heavy defeats. In the end, the failure of Theresa May's withdrawal agreement, and the failure of reaching her Conservative Party's majority in a June 2017 election, was her undoing. On 24 May 2019 she officially announced her resignation as prime minister.

After Theresa May resigned, Boris Johnson was elected as the Conservative Party leader and appointed prime minister in August 2019. After some political difficulties, Boris Johnson called a snap election for 12 December 2019 and won a majority government.

I have no doubt about Boris Johnson's ability to finalize Brexit, but I have some doubt about the wisdom of Brexit, and to what extent it will benefit the British and the European People. Also, I wonder how many times, if any, Boris Johnson has asked himself, "What if I'm wrong?"

Mother Russia

While the USA President Donald Trump was busy "Making America Great Again," all inward, the Russian President Vladimir Putin took a good look at Donald Trump's methods and decided to make Russia great again, but all outward. So, Vladimir Putin proceeds to make friends and allies with the nations that were rejected by Donald Trump. Following are some of the news items that reported Putin's actions:

March 2, 2018: The New Yorker: The relationship between Moscow and Tehran — once tactical militarily, coldly calculating diplomatically, and practical economically — has been converted into a growing strategic partnership. Vladimir Putin's relentless quest to make Russia a superpower again is part of it; Iran's goal is just to be a player again. Since President Trump took office, in 2017, Moscow and Tehran have shared increasingly common bonds: growing tensions with Washington and a quest to expand spheres of influence in the Middle East.

April 5, 2018: Daily News: Relations between Turkey and Russia are moving towards a "strategic partnership" status, even if they are still not officially described that way. The latest example of this is Turkey's purchase of S-400 missile defense systems from Russia. Turkey was only able to carry out the Afrin operation because Russia opened up air space there too, while cooperation between the two countries in the field of energy has been developing fast.

February 7, 2019: The Trumpet: German Foreign Minister Heiko Maas visited his Russian counterpart, Sergei Lavrov, in Moscow on January 18 to discuss, among other things, a new proposal to ensure unimpeded shipping through the Kerch Strait and Azov Sea. After the meeting, Maas flew to Ukraine to inform its leaders of the negotiations. The exclusive discussions between Germany and Russia, excluding Ukraine, reveal the close ties developing between these two powers.

June 5, 2019: CNBC: Chinese President Xi Jinping has described Russian President Vladimir Putin as his "best friend" during a three day state-visit to Russia. "In the past six years, we have met nearly 30 times. Russia is the country that I have visited the most times, and President Putin is my best friend and colleague," Xi said at a press conference Wednesday afternoon. Russia and China appear to be intent on strengthening their alliance and fostering deeper cooperation in the face of increased political and economic hostility from the U.S. That bid to strengthen bilateral ties continues this week with Xi visiting the country for top-level talks with Putin.

July 28, 2019: The Times of Israel: Targeting Israeli-Russian voters, Likud hangs massive picture of PM alongside Russian president, with the slogan 'Netanyahu: In a league of his own'

September 9, 2019: The Telegraph: France said the time had come to start bringing Russia in from the cold as senior ministers held talks in Moscow on Monday for the first time since the Russian annexation of Crimea from Ukraine.

Oct 14, 2019, Washington post: Russian President Vladimir Putin landed in Riyadh on Monday for his first state visit to Saudi Arabia and the United Arab Emirates in more than a decade, emphasizing not only coordination between three of the biggest oil producers in the world but also Moscow's growing influence in the Middle East. The timing may be especially fortuitous for Putin. President Trump's announcement last week that the United States would be pulling out of northeast Syria, as well as his equivocation over the conflict with Iran, has left many traditional U.S. allies in the region nervous.

October 17, 2019: The New York Times: As the United States withdraws from Syria, Russia is stepping in, running patrols to separate warring factions, striking deals and helping President Bashar al-Assad advance.

October 22, 2019: Moscow to host 40 leaders from the [African] continent in pursuit of allies and trading partners.

These are just a few of the reports that show how active Vladimir Putin is and has been to make Mother Russia great again by expanding her accumulation of allies.

Donald Trump wants desperately to make friends with Vladimir Putin, but Vladimir Putin doesn't mind taking advantage of Donald Trump's mistakes! Donald Trump would do well asking himself: "What if I'm wrong?"

Just think about this new strategy: during most of the twentieth century, Russia tried to convince other nations to become communistic. Now, during the twenty-first century, Russia is trying to ally herself with all these nations mentioned above without any thought of making them communistic. Economic considerations seem to play the bigger role now. This must surely be due to Vladimir Putin's political philosophy.

Pro-life vs. Pro-choice

Although I was brought up by Christian Baptist parents who were presumably pro-life, my strong leaning towards women's rights makes me sympathize with those who opt for pro-choice. I should also mention that during the Second World War years, a German soldier who was a practicing homeopath gave my mother a packet of an African herb, which he claimed could induce an abortion. He said it may come in handy if Russian soldiers raped any of my mother's women friends. I know she used the herb at least once successfully, when a neighbor lady's daughter was raped by a Russian soldier. So, I must assume that my mother supported pro-choice, regardless of her religious beliefs. On the other hand, I have been a lifelong admirer of Albert Schweitzer and his advocacy of reverence for life!

The expression "Reverence for Life" is a translation of the German phrase: "Ehrfurcht vor dem Leben." These words came to Albert Schweitzer on a boat trip on the Ogooué River in French Equatorial Africa (now Gabon), while searching for a universal concept of ethics for our time. Nevertheless, Albert

Arthur O.R. Thormann
≈

Schweitzer, who lived in Africa most of his life, also realized that nature has little regard for life, to wit: animals killing each other for their protein, or the many billions of male sperm and female ova that get lost before one of each combines to start a fetus. Most human beings also have no qualms having animals killed for their meals. Besides, human beings, with few exceptions, have no compunction killing each other to get what they or their leaders want, to wit: terrorism and all our terrible wars!

On October 6th 2019, I asked my female friends the following: Hi [friend]: Allow me to ask you a personal question: Are you pro-choice or pro-life oriented? Give me your reason, please. Here are some of the answers I received:

"I think every fetus should be born. Every fetus has a right to life. I had this when I was pregnant with my daughter; the doctor said there is a chance that she could be a child with special needs. But look at her now, her 18th Birthday is tomorrow. She is healthy and an amazing wonderful woman."

"I'm both (pro-life and pro-choice) depending on the situation. If you are raped, I can understand why, otherwise I think that all fetuses should have a chance to live, and there are lots of people who want children and can't have them, and these babies would be their little blessings."

"I feel like there is no right answer for this one. Personally, it is not something I could have ever done for my own moral reasons. But I know there are some situations for some woman where it may be necessary. Whether it is health reasons for mom or baby, or the circumstance in which she became pregnant, or a lot of other reasons."

"That is a question that always sparks conversations between groups. Where does life begin? Is it that moment when a cluster of cells forms? Or is it when consciousness is reached in the womb? Or when birth happens? I am pro-choice. I don't believe you should have a child if it is unwanted despite the circumstance. Not fair for you or the child. We all govern ourselves. A person has the right to get a tattoo or dye their hair and wear makeup. Why shouldn't this too be a decision that every woman can make based upon her views and values – whatever they may be!"

"I am pro-choice. I believe that women have a right to decide what happens to their own bodies. By banning abortion we put women at risk by driving them underground to look for a solution."

"Pro-choice leaves room for life, but pro-life rules out pro-choice."

When a woman wants to enjoy sex without getting pregnant, she uses one of the recognized preventions, which is also a pro-choice option, but even that is unacceptable to some religious fanatics. Of course, the argument can be made that life does not yet exist before a sperm and an ovum get together.

One interesting question is: does human life begin when an ovum is impregnated or does it begin any time later? According to the Wikipedia, in Eastern Mongolia, age is traditionally determined based on the number of full moons since conception for girls, and the number of new moons since birth for boys. So, if conception is when human life begins, then taking a human life would occur any time after conception, and that is where the dilemma is created for legislators, who must address abortion issues!

For politicians, the question of pro-life versus pro-choice comes down to morality. The politician who may support women's rights does not want to lose the vote of religious people who fight for pro-life. So, politicians waver on the question whether they support pro-choice or pro-life. This is not easily resolved. Yes, we have laws that make murder illegal, but even our lawmakers are divided on when such laws should apply to unborn children. The question "What if I'm wrong?" very much comes into play regarding this issue.

Nationalism

I was born in Germany at a time when nationalism was rampant. I'm not fool enough to believe that there are no benefits to nationalism, but I hope you will understand my skepticism, having lived my early years under National Socialism, led by the Führer, Adolf Hitler. I understand where Hitler was coming from on nationalism, but I also believe he should have asked himself, "what if I'm wrong?"

Rich Lowry's latest book, *The Case for Nationalism*, was released in November 2019. The following paragraphs are some of the published comments to market his book:

> It is one of our most honored clichés that America is an idea and not a nation. This is false. America is indisputably a nation, and one that desperately needs to protect its interests, its borders, and its identity.
> The Brexit vote and the election of Donald Trump swept nationalism to the forefront of the political debate. This is a good thing. Nationalism is usually assumed to be a dirty word, but it is a

foundation of democratic self-government and of international peace.

National Review editor Rich Lowry refutes critics on left and the right, reclaiming the term "nationalism" from those who equate it with racism, militarism, and fascism. He explains how nationalism is an American tradition, a thread that runs through such diverse leaders as Alexander Hamilton, Teddy Roosevelt, Martin Luther King, Jr., and Ronald Reagan.

In The Case for Nationalism, Lowry explains how nationalism was central to the American Project. It fueled the American Revolution and the ratification of the Constitution. It preserved the country during the Civil War. It led to the expansion of the American nation's territory and power, and eventually to our invaluable contribution to creating an international system of self-governing nations.

It's time to recover a healthy American nationalism, and especially a cultural nationalism that insists on the assimilation of immigrants and that protects our history, civic rituals, and traditions, which are under constant threat. At a time in which our nation is plagued by self-doubt and self-criticism, The Case for Nationalism offers a path for America to regain its national self-confidence and achieve continued greatness.

Following are some comments by one of our world renowned scientists and by our present world leaders on nationalism:

Albert Einstein: Nationalism is an infantile disease, the measles of mankind. Our world faces a crisis as yet unperceived by those possessing power to make great decisions for good or evil.
(www.federalunion.org.uk)

Justin Trudeau: Trudeau warns of dangers of nationalist leaders at historic armistice gathering. Nov. 12th 2018 (www.nationalobserver.com)

Angela Merkel: Nationalism and egoism must never have a chance again in Europe. Nov. 13th 2018 (www.europarl.europa.eu)

Emmanuel Macron: Macron rebukes nationalism as Trump observes Armistice Day Nov. 12, 2018 (www.cnn.com)

Boris Johnson: Johnson and the right-wing Tories in Cabinet are English nationalists who hope to turn UK into a US 'colony', a country where EU regulations are replaced by limited welfare, minimum standards, low taxes and low pay, writes Henry McLeish. Aug. 6, 2019 (www.scotsman.com)

Donald Trump: Donald Trump has used his address to the UN general assembly to deliver a nationalist manifesto, denouncing "globalism" and illegal immigration and promoting patriotism as a cure for the world's ills. Sep. 24, 2019 (www.theguardian.com)

Obviously, the majority of our world leaders are opposed to nationalism, per se, but they might well be in favor of some benefits of nationalism. However, all of them should ask themselves, "What if I'm wrong?"

Climate Change

If we can believe what a large number of scientists are trying to tell us, the Earth is seriously into climate change. However, US President Donald Trump believes climate change is just a hoax. What if he is wrong?

Climate change occurs when changes in Earth's climate system result in new weather patterns that remain in place for an extended period of time. This length of time can be as short as a few decades; more recently since the industrial revolution, the climate has increasingly been affected by human activities driving global warming. (Wikipedia)

Over the course of three years, NASA flew a plane carrying gas-imaging equipment above California and made a discovery that surprised even the state's own environmental agencies: A handful of operations are responsible for the vast majority of methane emissions. In a report published in Nature on Wednesday, scientists estimated that 10% of the places releasing methane – including landfills, natural gas facilities, and dairy farms – are responsible for more than half of the state's total emissions. And a fraction of the 272,000 sources surveyed – just 0.2% – account for as much as 46%.

Politicians who take these scientists seriously are trying to stop or even reverse our climate change. One way is to promote the use of electric cars.

Electricity can be economically produced through natural gas, which is also ecologically safer than burning the fossil fuel used by the majority of our present cars. However, people are still hesitant to switch to electric cars because of the unavailability of electric charging stations to charge the battery of these cars. But some governments are seriously promoting the production of charging stations.

Here is a news report by the Thomson Reuters Foundation, November 4, 2019: Germany should have one million charging stations for electric cars by 2030, Chancellor Angela Merkel said in a video message on Sunday, ahead of meetings on Monday with the car industry on how to speed the move to low-emission battery-powered vehicles. "For this purpose, we want to create a million charging points by the year 2030 and the industry will have to participate in this effort, that is what we will be talking about," Merkel said. Germany now has just 20,000 public charging points. Merkel also said the government aimed to preserve jobs making cars and parts, since it is becoming clear that fewer employees are needed to construct electric cars than conventional ones. Stephan Weil, the prime minister in Lower Saxony, where Volkswagen is based, said he wanted to see commitments for 100,000 public charging points in place by 2021. Apart from electric alternatives to gasoline and diesel-driven cars, the German government will also explore those run on hydrogen fuel cells.

Other governments around the world are also actively promoting various methods to reduce climate change. The Canadian government is promoting carbon pricing, clean electricity, transportation, buildings, innovation, and the Pan-Canadian Framework to combat climate change. New Zealand has passed a law that aims to make the country almost carbon neutral by 2050. Farmers, who bring in a large portion of foreign income, will be given some flexibility.

According to the Wikipedia, as countries develop more strategies to promote clean and renewable energy and ways of living, places within the United States such as California are making reforms. In 2016, the state of California passed Senate Bill 32, which strengthens the need to withhold the state from emitting excess carbon. Although Donald Trump has tried to remove the United States from the Paris Agreement, other states such as New York have been creating greener spaces by installing more solar panels and creating "green building" which mitigate pollution in an effort to make New York City "cleaner." Countries are making large efforts to fight and reduce the effects of climate change; however, in order to see improvements, more countries with large CO_2 emissions, such as China and India, will need to reform and cut emissions by large percentages.

As per the ClimateActionTracker, September 19, 2019, China is the world's largest greenhouse gas emitter, and its actions both at home and abroad have an enormous impact on global greenhouse gas emissions. Discouragingly, increased fossil-fuel consumption drove an estimated 2.3% increase in Chinese CO_2 emissions in 2018, a second year of growth, after emissions had appeared to level out between 2014 and 2016. China is simultaneously, and almost paradoxically, the world's largest consumer of coal and the largest solar technology manufacturer.

As per Economic Times, August 26, 2019, India has said that it will finalize its long-term plan strategies for development that result in lower levels of carbon dioxide and other greenhouse gas emissions by 2020. India also said that it will increase its climate pledges.

Hopefully, the efforts of these countries to reduce or eliminate climate change will soon be effective.

Healthcare

People are concerned about their healthcare, and so they should be. Fortunately, healthcare in Canada is looked after by federal and provincial governments.

To quote the Wikipedia: Healthcare in Canada is delivered through the provincial and territorial systems of publicly funded health care, informally called Medicare. It is guided by the provisions of the Canada Health Act of 1984, and is universal. However, 30 percent of Canadians' healthcare is paid for through the private sector. This mostly goes towards services not covered or partially covered by Medicare, such as prescription drugs, dentistry, and optometry. In common with many other developed countries, Canada is experiencing a cost increase due to a demographic shift towards an older population, with more retirees and fewer people of working age. In 2006, the average age was 39.5 years; within twelve years it had risen to 42.4 years, with a life expectancy of 81.1 years. 80 percent of Canadian adults self-report having at least one major risk factor for chronic disease; smoking, physical inactivity, unhealthy eating or excessive alcohol use. Canada has one of the highest rates of adult obesity among Organization for Economic Co-operation and Development (OECD) countries attributing to approximately 2.7 million cases of diabetes (types 1 and 2 combined). Four chronic diseases: cancer, cardiovascular diseases, respiratory diseases, and diabetes account for 65 percent of deaths in Canada. In 2017 Canada ranked above the average on OECD indicators for wait-times and access to care, with average scores for quality of care and use of resources.

Notwithstanding Canada's example of healthcare provisions, its neighbor, the United States of America, seems to have extraordinary problems to provide an acceptable healthcare system. Healthcare facilities are largely owned and operated by private sector businesses. 58% of community hospitals in the United States are non-profit, 21% are government owned, and 21% are for-profit. Healthcare coverage is provided through a combination of private health insurance and public health coverage (e.g., Medicare, Medicaid). The United States does not have a universal healthcare program, unlike some other countries. Prohibitively high cost is the primary reason our American friends have problems accessing health care. The number of people without health insurance coverage in the United States is one of the primary concerns raised by advocates of health care reform. Lack of health insurance is associated with increased mortality, about sixty thousand preventable deaths per year, depending on the study. US President Donald Trump said, "We will not rest until Americans have the healthcare system they need and deserve, a system that finally puts American patients first." In touting her new plan to pay for Medicare for All, Sen. Elizabeth Warren, candidate for the 2020 US presidency, has argued that she won't raise taxes on the middle class (to pay for her plan of healthcare).

According to the Commonwealth Fund, which regularly ranks the health systems of a handful of developed countries, the best countries for health care are the United Kingdom, the Netherlands, and Australia, and the lowest performer is the United States, even though it spends the most. "And this is consistent across 20 years," said the Commonwealth Fund's president, David Blumenthal, at the Spotlight Health Festival, which is co-hosted by the Aspen Institute and The Atlantic. Blumenthal laid out three reasons why the United States lags behind its peers so consistently. It all comes down to:

1. A lack of insurance coverage: More than 27 million people in the United States were uninsured in 2016—nearly a tenth of the population—often because they can't afford

coverage, live in a state that didn't expand Medicaid, or are undocumented.

2. Administrative inefficiency: According to the Commonwealth Fund's most recent report, in the United States, doctors and patients are wasting time on billing and insurance claims. While insurance coverage in general is great, it's not ideal that different insurance plans cover different treatments and procedures, forcing doctors to spend precious hours coordinating with insurance companies to provide care.

3. Underperforming primary care: "We have a very disorganized, fragmented, inefficient, and under-resourced primary care system," Blumenthal added. "Many primary-care physicians struggle to receive relevant clinical information from specialists and hospitals, complicating efforts to provide seamless, coordinated care."

Together, these reasons help explain why U.S. life expectancy has, for the first time since the 1960s, recently gone down for two years in a row.

Providing adequate and efficient healthcare must be high on the agenda of politicians of every nation. Both doctors and patients must be consulted. Furthermore, when it comes to healthcare, politicians must ask themselves, "What if we're wrong?" – An important question when it comes to healthcare.

Disarmament

When nations reach a point of over armament, they must start thinking in terms of disarmament, especially as far as weapons of mass destruction are concerned.

In a highly symbolic visit to Nagasaki, one of the two Japanese cities devastated by nuclear strikes during the closing days of World War II in August 1945, Pope Francis said nuclear weapons were "not the answer" for global security, peace, and stability. "Convinced as I am that a world without nuclear weapons is possible and necessary, I ask political leaders not to forget that these weapons cannot protect us from current threats to national and international security," Francis said in Nagasaki on Sunday. "Peace and international stability are incompatible with attempts to build upon the fear of mutual destruction or the threat of total annihilation," Francis noted. "They can be achieved only on the basis of a global ethic of solidarity and cooperation."[*]

I find myself in agreement with Pope Francis on many issues. The idea of hoarding huge numbers of nuclear weapons seems illogical and irresponsible.

---

[*] As reported in the Deutsche Welle on November 24, 2019.

According to the Wikipedia, eight sovereign states have publicly announced successful detonation of nuclear weapons. Five are considered to be nuclear-weapon states (NWS) under the terms of the Treaty on the Non-Proliferation of Nuclear Weapons (NPT). In order of acquisition of nuclear weapons these are the United States, Russia (the successor state to the Soviet Union), the United Kingdom, France, and China. Since the NPT entered into force in 1970, three states that were not parties to the Treaty have conducted overt nuclear tests, namely India, Pakistan, and North Korea. North Korea had been a party to the NPT but withdrew in 2003. Israel is also generally understood to have nuclear weapons, but does not acknowledge it, maintaining a policy of deliberate ambiguity, and is not known definitively to have conducted a nuclear test. Israel is estimated to possess somewhere between 75 and 400 nuclear warheads. One possible motivation for nuclear ambiguity is deterrence with minimum political cost.

Can you imagine any one of these countries using a nuclear weapon to start a war? If not, why hoard them? The initial notion was, let's get a nuclear weapon to defend ourselves against counties who may use nuclear weapons against us. Does that sound reasonable? I do not think so, but you are welcome to disagree with me. Except for the nuclear weapons that were dropped on Japan in August, 1945, no other ones were used to start or end a war. The logic for this is obvious: it would truly be a war to end all wars, because no one would survive to start another war! Countries with nuclear weapons must seriously ask themselves the question before using them, "What if we're wrong?"

US President Donald Trump, in a combative debut speech to the UN General Assembly, threatened the "total destruction" of North Korea if it does not abandon its drive towards nuclear weapons. However, I seriously doubt his intentions of destruction. I think he said this as a negotiating ploy. Donald Trump is too smart to start a nuclear war.

In a report from Moscow On February 20, 2019, the Russian President Vladimir Putin warned the Trump administration against basing intermediate-range missiles in Europe, saying that Moscow would respond by deploying new weapons of its own that could directly target Washington. Although the threat did not mark a change in Russian doctrine, it raised the ante in what could be a new arms race between the two countries. Russia and the United States already have stockpiles of hundreds of nuclear-armed missiles capable of reaching each other's territory, a vestige of Cold War hostilities. But Putin's annual state of the nation address to both houses of parliament and his government ministries was a warning that a nuclear-armed standoff between the two countries appears in danger of returning. Again, I think he said this as a negotiating ploy. Vladimir Putin, too, is too smart to start a nuclear war.

However, some smaller country with nuclear weapons, with an irresponsible idiot leading it, could well use these weapons thoughtlessly! And that is where the larger countries' dilemma comes in for disarmament. They don't trust countries like North Korea and Pakistan, and Iran, for that matter, because Iran is making serious efforts to become a nuclear power. An Iran nuclear deal framework was reached in 2015 between the Islamic Republic of Iran and the United States, the United Kingdom, Russia, France, China, Germany, and the European Union. However, in May 2018 President Trump announced the US is withdrawing from the deal. This upset the other nations of the deal, who felt that President Trump should ask himself, "What if I'm wrong?"

Immigration

I am an immigrant to Canada. To be allowed into the country, my background was checked, my health was checked, and I had to have a financial backer. Satisfied, Canada issued me an immigration card that I had to present at my port of entry, Halifax. This is called a legal immigration!

The reason why so many countries have immigration problems is because some, if not most, potential immigrants cannot pass the country's immigration requirements and decide to immigrate illegally.

An annoying illegal immigration problem occurs in the southern United States of America, where immigrants come into the United States from Mexico. US President Donald Trump wanted to stop this immigration by building a wall between the United States and Mexico — in fact, he wanted Mexico to pay for this wall, because Mexico was unable or unwilling to stop this illegal immigration.

The problem becomes more complex when illegal immigrants have children that were born in the United States! Theoretically, anyone born in a country is automatically a citizen of that country, but if the parents were illegal immigrants of that country, the country may refuse to grant their children a citizenship as well. In that case, human rights issues become involved.

To make matters even more complex, consider that the farmers of the southern United States of America actually invited and sanctioned these illegal immigrants, in order to obtain cheap labor, and these farmers are opposed to rejecting or exporting these immigrants for the same reason.

There are about twelve million illegal immigrants in the USA, about 3.6% of the population, and these immigrants must be cared for, such as education, health care, corrections, and welfare.

Every country has illegal immigrants — some of the countries not even aware of the extent. Then, you have countries like the United Kingdom, who allowed immigration due to their membership in the European Union, and when this became objectionable they issued a referendum to decide whether to continue with this policy or leave the European Union. There were other issues, to be sure, but this was one of the main issues, triggered by the migration from the Middle East. In Germany, Chancellor Angela Merkel wanted to allow one million of these migrants per year, and the German people told her, "Enough is enough," and reduced her party of valuable seats in the next election, which caused her to give notice of her retirement in 2021. She would have been well advised to ask herself, "what if I'm wrong?"

Emigration is the opposite of immigration. When the United Kingdom transferred Hong Kong to China on July 1, 1997, wealthy people resident in Hong Kong decided to emigrate to safer havens, like Vancouver, BC, Canada. This created an inflationary spiral of real estate prices, which the government eventually tried to control with a special tax. For example, a new 20% tax was added to the Property Transfer Tax when a purchaser, who is not a Canadian citizen or permanent resident, purchases residential real estate property in Metro Vancouver. Furthermore, doctors are often in disagreement with government health care systems. For example, the Canadian healthcare system is guided by the provisions of the Canada Health Act adopted in 1984, and some Canadian doctors disagreed with the Canadian healthcare system and decided to emigrate to other countries, mainly the United States of America. The exodus of a country's professionals is always a great loss, and governments should do their best to avoid it and ask themselves, "What if we're wrong?" Here is what the McGill Journal of Medicine reported on the Canadian province of Quebec passing of Bill 20:

The current version of Bill 20, formally titled, "An Act to enact the Act to promote access to family medicine and specialized medicine services and to amend various legislative provisions relating to assisted procreation," was passed on November 10, 2015 amidst great controversy. Due to the passing of Bill 20 in a top-down fashion, many family doctors are contemplating to leave the province to practice medicine in other provinces.

Other emigrations occur because of political disagreements. For example, during the 1930s, many Jewish people in Germany saw the handwriting on the wall with Hitler's anti-Semitic regime and decided to emigrate to other countries. Of course, Hitler not only ignored but welcomed Germany's loss of respected Jewish people. In fact, Hitler encouraged the Jewish peoples' emigration. For example, in January 1933, some 522,000 Jews lived in Germany, and over 58% emigrated from Germany during the first six years of the Nazi dictatorship.

Then, you have the massive exodus from Syria due to its ongoing multi-sided civil war since March 15, 2011.

Immigration will always cause some problems but also results in many benefits for all concerned.

Gun Laws

Fortunately, most countries have gun laws to control and or restrict the ownership and use of firearms. I owned some firearms, mostly for hunting, during the 1960s and 1970s, but when I decided to stop hunting, I sold my firearms. I saw only risks in keeping them. The following gun-law information comes mainly from the internet, mainly the Wikipedia, to whom I am an occasional financial contributor.

Although Mexico and Guatemala both have a constitutional right to bear arms, the US is in a league of its own, because it is the only country without any restrictions on gun ownership in its constitution. Here is what the US Bill of Rights Second Amendment stipulates: "A well regulated Militia, being necessary to the security of a free State, the right of the people to keep and bear Arms, shall not be infringed."

In the US, access to guns is controlled by law under a number of federal statutes. These laws regulate the manufacture, trade, possession, transfer, record keeping, transport, and destruction of firearms, ammunition, and firearms accessories. In addition to federal gun laws, all state governments and some local governments have their own laws.

Mexico has extremely restrictive laws regarding gun possession. There is only one gun store in the entire country, and it takes months of paperwork to have a chance at purchasing one legally. While it is true that Mexico possesses strict gun laws, where most types and calibers are reserved to military and law enforcement, the acquisition and ownership of certain firearms and ammunition remains a constitutional right to all Mexican citizens and foreign legal residents.

Gun legislation in Canada is largely about licensing and registration of firearms, including air guns. In 1969, laws classified firearms as "non-restricted," "restricted," and "prohibited." Starting in 1979, people who wished to acquire firearms were required to obtain a firearms acquisition certificate (FAC) from their local police agency.

The European Firearms Directive is a law of the European Union which sets minimum standards regarding civilian firearms acquisition and possession that EU Member States must implement into their national legal systems. The Member States are free to adopt more stringent rules, which lead to differences in the extent of citizens' legal access to firearms within different EU countries.

In the United Kingdom, access by the general

public to firearms is subject to some of the strictest control measures in the world. Laws differ and are generally less restrictive in Northern Ireland. Concerns have been raised over the availability of illegal firearms. Members of the public may own sporting rifles and shotguns, subject to licensing, but handguns were effectively banned after the Dunblane school massacre in 1996 with the exception of Northern Ireland.

In Germany, access to guns is controlled by the German Weapons Act (German: Waffengesetz) which adheres to the European Firearms Directive, first enacted in 1972, and superseded by the law of 2003, in force as of 2016. This federal statute regulates the handling of firearms and ammunition as well as acquisition, storage, commerce and maintenance of firearms.

In France, to buy a weapon, in line with the European Firearms Directive, a hunting license or a shooting sport license is necessary depending on the type, function, and magazine capacity of the weapon.

Gun control in Italy incorporates the political and regulatory aspects of firearms usage in the country within the framework of the European Union's Firearm Directive. Different types of gun licenses can be obtained from the national police authorities.

The regulation of guns in Spain is highly

restrictive. The bearing of arms by civilians is not considered a right but a privilege that may be granted by the government if legal conditions are met. Firearms licenses for personal security are restricted to those who can prove that a real danger to their security exists.

Russian citizens over 18 years of age can obtain a firearms license after attending gun-safety classes and passing a federal test and background check. The license is valid for five years and may be renewed. Firearms may be acquired for self-defense, hunting, or sports activities.

In some countries, for example China, Japan, and Myanmar, only very limited groups of people can own firearms. In few countries, including Cambodia, Eritrea, and Solomon Islands, ownership of firearms is completely prohibited.

I think the ownership of a firearm should mainly be a personal decision, but controlled by gun laws, whether used for sports, for hunting, or for protection, but one must always ask himself or herself regarding the ownership of a firearm, "What if I'm wrong?"

The Economy

My main involvement with the economy was in the construction business, trying to meet tough competition. To lower our sales prices, we had to cut our overhead, demand more output from our workforces, and try to buy our materials cheaper – all of this to meet a tough economy. After including these savings, if our competition still beat us, we asked ourselves, "What if we're wrong?" and we examined our cuts again. For example, when cutting overhead, we may have decided to lay off office workers and, thus, also reduce our production. But a better solution would have been to find a way to increase the production of our office workers. The same applies to field workers.

To increase the production of the workforce, we decided to give high-productive workers a 5-10% pay increase and lay off less productive workers, replacing them with more productive ones. Eventually, our entire workforce was paid 5-10% above the average in the industry, but the productivity of the workforce was close to 20% above the average. This was a more certain way for us to beat the competitive economy we were facing. Businesses and individuals have the choice to place themselves on either side of the averages, but governments do not have this choice, they must deal with the averages.

We expect our governments to stimulate the economy, to create ample employment for us; also, to help us use our resources wisely to produce goods and services efficiently and to make us globally competitive; furthermore, we expect our governments to manage the economy to increase the output of goods and services over time; then, we expect them to allocate the wealth produced fairly and equitably, and provide us with social programs as needed; our governments must also manage the economy to achieve relatively stable prices over time, and manage our resources and the environment for our benefit and the benefit of future generations. It is impossible to accomplish all of this, you say. No, not impossible, but a tall order, which we expect of our governments. And what if our governments go wrong? Then we just have to elect different governments.

So, how do our governments go about to accomplish these seemingly impossible tasks? Money dictates the path of an economy, and that is where our governments play a vital part. There is usually a state bank involved. In Canada, it is The Bank of Canada, which undertakes its role to create the right monetary conditions for growth and stability of the economy.

Chartered in 1934 under the Bank of Canada Act, it is responsible for formulating Canada's monetary policy, and for the promotion of a safe and sound financial system within Canada. The Bank of Canada is the sole issuing authority of Canadian banknotes, provides banking services and money management for the government, and loans money to Canadian financial institutions. The contract to produce the banknotes has been held by the Canadian Bank Note Company since 1935.

Just as businesses and consumers are involved with the supply and demand of goods and services, so is the Bank of Canada involved with the monetary supply and demand, which can also influence the supply and demand of goods and services. For example, the Bank of Canada can increase the supply of printed money by buying Canada bonds from investors in the market place. This new supply of money, if too much, can chase the supply of goods and services, and thus increase their prices and causing inflation. The same applies in reverse, causing deflation. Of course, normally the Bank of Canada would be careful to keep inflation to a manageable level of two percent, which stimulates the economy – deflation can harm the economy.

Another function of the Bank of Canada is to

control Canada's interest rates. The Bank of Canada can generally determine Canada's interest rates because it is the principle lender of money to chartered banks and other lenders, such as credit unions. The bank of Canada interest rate is called the bank rate and can be changed at any time. If the bank rate is lowered, other lenders can also lower the interest rate they charge their borrowers and, thus, boost spending, and economic activity will pick up. Conversely, if the Bank of Canada wishes to reduce spending, it can increase the bank rate. However, when interest rates increase, they can also influence the Canadian dollar's foreign exchange rate, because more foreign investors will wish to buy Canadian investments, thus increasing the demand for the Canadian dollar.

In addition to monetary suasion, the Bank of Canada also uses moral suasion to persuade the financial industry to move in certain directions. For example, recently the Bank of Canada expressed concern to the banks about overheating house prices and the household debt level in Canada.

Similar controls also exist with the United States Department of the Treasury, the Bank of England, and the European Central Bank. It is easy to see who controls our economies and how they are controlled, but the question, "What if we're wrong?" must often occur at these controlling banks and treasuries.

Foreign Policy

Foreign policy is a government's strategy in dealing with other nations. I think diplomacy should play a major part of foreign policy. A country has friends that it wishes to maintain and enemies that it wishes to transform.

The stated aims of the foreign policy of the Donald Trump administration include a focus on security, by fighting terrorists abroad and strengthening border defenses and immigration controls; an expansion of the U.S. military; an "America First" approach to trade; and diplomacy whereby "old enemies become friends".

According to CNN, Trump's talks with world leaders, in public, on the phone, and in private, have frequently dropped jaws to the ground either for their unprecedented nature, their awkward details, or their instant reversal of US policy. Trump can become frustrated with world leaders, as he did with then Australian Prime Minister Malcolm Turnbull. Trump didn't want to honor an agreement between Turnbull and President Barack Obama regarding refugees. After a long and contentious back-and-forth, Trump told

Turnbull, "I have had it. I have been making these calls all day and this is the most unpleasant call all day. Putin was a pleasant call. This is ridiculous."

Trump criticized then-UK Prime Minister Theresa May during an interview with a British tabloid while he was in England in July of 2018. "I told her how to do it," he said of May's approach on Brexit at the time, according to audio posted by the Sun. "That will be up to her to say. But I told her how to do it. She wanted to go a different route."

He also had a tense call with Canadian Prime Minister Justin Trudeau about tariffs in June of 2017. The White House described that call as "amicable." The Canadian version of the readout suggested Trudeau disputed "baseless" claims by the US Department of Commerce about Canadian lumber and described him as promising to "vigorously" defend Canada. But it's another meeting with Trudeau that is more telling. Trump told supporters at a fundraiser in Missouri in 2018 that he insisted during one meeting with Trudeau that the US has a trade deficit with Canada -- that it buys more from Canada than it sells to the country. Trudeau was right that the US has a trade surplus with Canada. Trump later argued on Twitter, despite the facts published by his commerce department, that there is a deficit.

New York Times reported March 2018: President

Trump told donors on Saturday that China's president, Xi Jinping, was now "president for life," and added: "I think it's great. Maybe we'll want to give that a shot someday." The comment was made behind closed doors, and appeared to be in jest, but Chinese analysts took them seriously.

The New Yorker reported December 2018 that at a July NATO summit in Brussels, Angela Merkel, the German Chancellor, proposed a closed-door emergency meeting. The emergency was Donald Trump. Minutes earlier, the President had arrived late to a session where the Presidents of Ukraine and Georgia were making their case to join NATO. Trump interrupted their presentation and unleashed a verbal assault on the members of the alliance, calling them deadbeats and free riders on American power. His barrage centered on Merkel, Europe's longest-serving democratic leader, "You, Angela," Trump chided Merkel.

USA Today reported November 2018: After spending a weekend at commemorations for the end of World War I, President Donald Trump waited until he returned to the White House to go after France's Emmanuel Macron on trade, defense, nationalism, and Macron's low approval ratings. French officials said Trump's comments were riddled with errors.

The Scotsman reported June 2019: Scotland's

long-standing ties with the US will "transcend" the current freeze in relations between Donald Trump's administration and the SNP Government at Holyrood (led by Prime Minister Nicola Sturgeon).

The Guardian reported August 2019: Trump's affinity for Putin and other autocrats has long drawn criticism, for upending the norms of US foreign policy and alienating traditional allies. But his pro-Russia posture in Biarritz left former diplomats and national security experts baffled and sounding fresh alarms.

Evening Standard reported October 31, 2019: Donald Trump has claimed Jeremy Corbyn as prime minister would be "so bad" for the UK as he urged Nigel Farage and Boris Johnson to strike an election pact and make an "unstoppable force".

The Atlantic reported November 2019: Donald Trump has claimed Boris Johnson as his bumbling, blond-haired mini-me from across the water.

In all his criticisms, and praise for that matter, of foreign leaders, it would surprise me if Donald Trump ever asked himself the important question, "What if I'm wrong?"

Hong Kong

Hong Kong has already been inhabited since the Old Stone Age, going back millions of years. It started as a farming and fishing village and eventually became part of the Qin Dynasty circa 221 BC. Early Hong Kong inhabitants enjoyed a relatively nutritious diet and practiced a religion based on cosmology. Cantonese-speaking newcomers looked down upon the original inhabitants, and most of the originals were shunted off to sea to live on boats. Today's fisher people emerged from this persecuted group.

When the Qing Dynasty (1644-1911) took over from the moribund Ming Dynasty, the Triads, originally founded as a patriotic secret society, dedicated themselves to overthrow the Qing and restore the Ming, but degenerated over the centuries as Hong Kong's own version of the Mafia. Today's Triads still recite an oath of allegiance to Ming, but their loyalty is to the dollar.

Eventually, Hong Kong was boosted by the influx of the Hakka, the guest people, who moved in during the 18th century up to the mid-19th century. Regular trade between China and Europe began in

1557, when Portuguese navigators set up a base in Macau, 65 km west of Hong Kong. Dutch and French traders followed, and British ships appeared as early as 1685 from the East India Company. However, there was a European trade deficit with China until the British disgraced China with opium.

China, seeing its silver draining from the country to pay for opium, which the British could supply in quantity from the poppy fields in India, and being alarmed by the opium addiction of its population, soon banned the opium trade. A British expeditionary force of 4000 men departed to extract reparations and secure favorable trade with the Chinese government, at what became known as the First Opium War, which began in 1840. The British forces besieged Guangzhou and then sailed north. The force threatened Beijing, and the emperor sent his envoy, Qi Shan, to negotiate a settlement. In exchange for the British withdrawal from Northern China, Qi agreed to cede Hong Kong to Britain, and in January of 1841 a British naval landing party hoisted the British flag at Possession Point, Hong Kong. Thus, Hong Kong became a British colony until 1997, although it was briefly occupied by Japan 1941 to 1945 during WWII.

In 1949, when the Communists came to power in China, many people were afraid Chinese forces would overrun Hong Kong, but, although the Chinese government still denounced the unequal treaties with Britain, it also recognized Hong Kong's importance to its national economy. Hong Kong consists of three main regions, one of them the New Territories, making up 86.2% of Hong Kong with half its population. The New Territories were leased from China by Britain in 1898 for 99 years, and upon the expiry of the lease in 1997, Britain transferred sovereignty of the New Territories to the People's Republic of China, together with the Qing-ceded the Hong Kong Island and the Kowloon Peninsula.

After the takeover in 1997, Hong Kong became a special administration region of the People's Republic of China, and unlike other provinces of China, it has certain political and economic freedoms. However, more recently Hong Kong became concerned with the intensifying economic inequality and with Beijing's efforts to encroach on the city's political systems. Hong Kong manages its affairs based on "one country, two systems," a national unification policy developed by Deng Xiaoping in the 1980s, intended to reintegrate Taiwan, Hong Kong, and Macau with sovereign China. The Chinese Communist Party does not preside over Hong Kong as it does over the mainland provinces, but Beijing still exerts considerable influence over Hong Kong through its loyalists. Furthermore, Beijing maintains authority to interpret Hong Kong's Basic Law, a power it has used few times since 1997. Under the Basic Law, Hong Kongers are also guaranteed freedom of the press, expression, assembly, and religion. But Beijing maintains control over its diplomacy and defense.

Hong Kong's economic power has diminished significantly since 1997 relative to mainland China, its GDP falling from 16% to less than 3% in 2017. At the same time, Hong Kong relies heavily on the mainland.

China is reluctant to allow Hong Kong to develop into a full-fledged democracy. Ambiguities in the Basic Law heighten this tension. In the most recent election, only Beijing nominating committee vetted candidates were allowed to run, and Carrie Lam, an establishment candidate, won the race in 2017.

Beijing increased its efforts to reign in political dissention starting in 2014, but tension with Beijing came to the fore again in the summer of 2019, protesting a legislative proposal that would have allowed extraditions to mainland China, but Carrie Lam withdrew the bill in September. Nevertheless, protesters are still demanding electoral reform and an investigation into police violence. Beijing is also aware of outside opinions regarding the treatment of its protesters, which makes the protesters more daring. Certainly, Beijing is not asking itself, "What if we're wrong?" and neither are the protesters.

Appendix: Assisted Suicide

I'm a believer in assisted suicide, which is suicide that is assisted by a physician or other healthcare provider. Once it is determined that the person's situation qualifies under the assisted suicide laws for that place, the physician's assistance is usually limited to writing a prescription for a lethal dose of drugs.

In many jurisdictions, helping a person die by suicide is a crime. People who support legalizing assisted suicide want the people who assist in a voluntary suicide to be exempt from criminal prosecution for manslaughter or similar crimes. Assisted suicide is legal in some countries, under certain circumstances, including Canada, Belgium, the Netherlands, Luxembourg, Colombia, Switzerland, parts of the United States, and Victoria, Australia. In countries that allow assisted suicide the conditions for its performance are usually fairly strict, like certifiable brain death, or terminal illness with unbearable and uncontrollable pain.

Nevertheless, regardless of what the law allows, some people are dead against assisted suicide, usually based on some religious belief. So be it, if they prefer the excruciating pain of a terminal disease over death. Merriam Webster's dictionary calls suicide the act or an instance of taking one's own life voluntarily and intentionally. Also, suicide is sometimes referred to as self-murder, and, as murder of course, it is considered unlawful by most people and nations. However, anyone who even remotely sanctions assisted suicide must certainly ask him- or herself: "What if I'm wrong?"

I included the topic of assisted suicide in this book, albeit as an appendix, because it is also a hot political issue in many countries.

About the Author

Arthur Thormann was born 7 April 1934 in Berlin, Germany. He came to Canada at age 17 in 1951, and became a naturalized Canadian in November 1957. He loves Canadians more than any other people, and thinks Canadians are probably the most democratic people in the world.

Arthur O. R. Thormann

≈